SPOTLIGHT ON NATURE
DOLPHIN

MELISSA GISH

CREATIVE EDUCATION · CREATIVE PAPERBACKS

Published by Creative Education and Creative Paperbacks
P.O. Box 227, Mankato, Minnesota 56002
Creative Education and Creative Paperbacks are imprints
of The Creative Company
www.thecreativecompany.us

Design by Chelsey Luther; production by Joe Kahnke
Art direction by Rita Marshall
Printed in the United States of America

Photographs by Alamy (Arco Images GmbH, Helmut Corneli, Cultura
Creative [RF], Natalia Pryanishnikova, robertharding, Stephen Frink Collec-
tion, Steve Bloom Images), Getty Images (Jonathan Bird/Photolibrary, Cat
Gennaro/Moment Open, Jeff Rotman/Photolibrary, Gerard Soury/Oxford
Scientific, Wild Horizon/Universal Images Group), iStockphoto (alexxx1981,
DebraMcGuire, federicoriz, PhotographerOlympus), Minden Pictures (Rich-
ard Herrmann, Alex Mustard/NPL, Kevin Schafer), Shutterstock (arka38,
Willyam Bradberry, Rich Carey, Andrea Izzotti, Pantera)

Library of Congress Cataloging-in-Publication Data
Names: Gish, Melissa, author.
Title: Dolphin / Melissa Gish.
Series: Spotlight on nature.
Includes index.
Summary: A detailed chronology of developmental milestones drives this life
study of dolphins, including their habitats, physical features, and conservation
measures taken to protect these marine mammals.
Identifiers: LCCN 2018041001 / ISBN 978-1-64026-180-8 (hardcover) /
ISBN 978-1-62832-743-4 (pbk) / ISBN 978-1-64000-298-2 (eBook)
Subjects: LCSH: Atlantic spotted dolphin—Bahamas—Mayaguana Island—
Juvenile literature. / Mayaguana Island (Bahamas)—Juvenile literature. /
Dolphins—Bahamas.
Classification: LCC QL737.C432 G567 2019 / DDC 599.53097296—dc23

First Edition HC 9 8 7 6 5 4 3 2 1
First Edition PBK 9 8 7 6 5 4 3 2 1

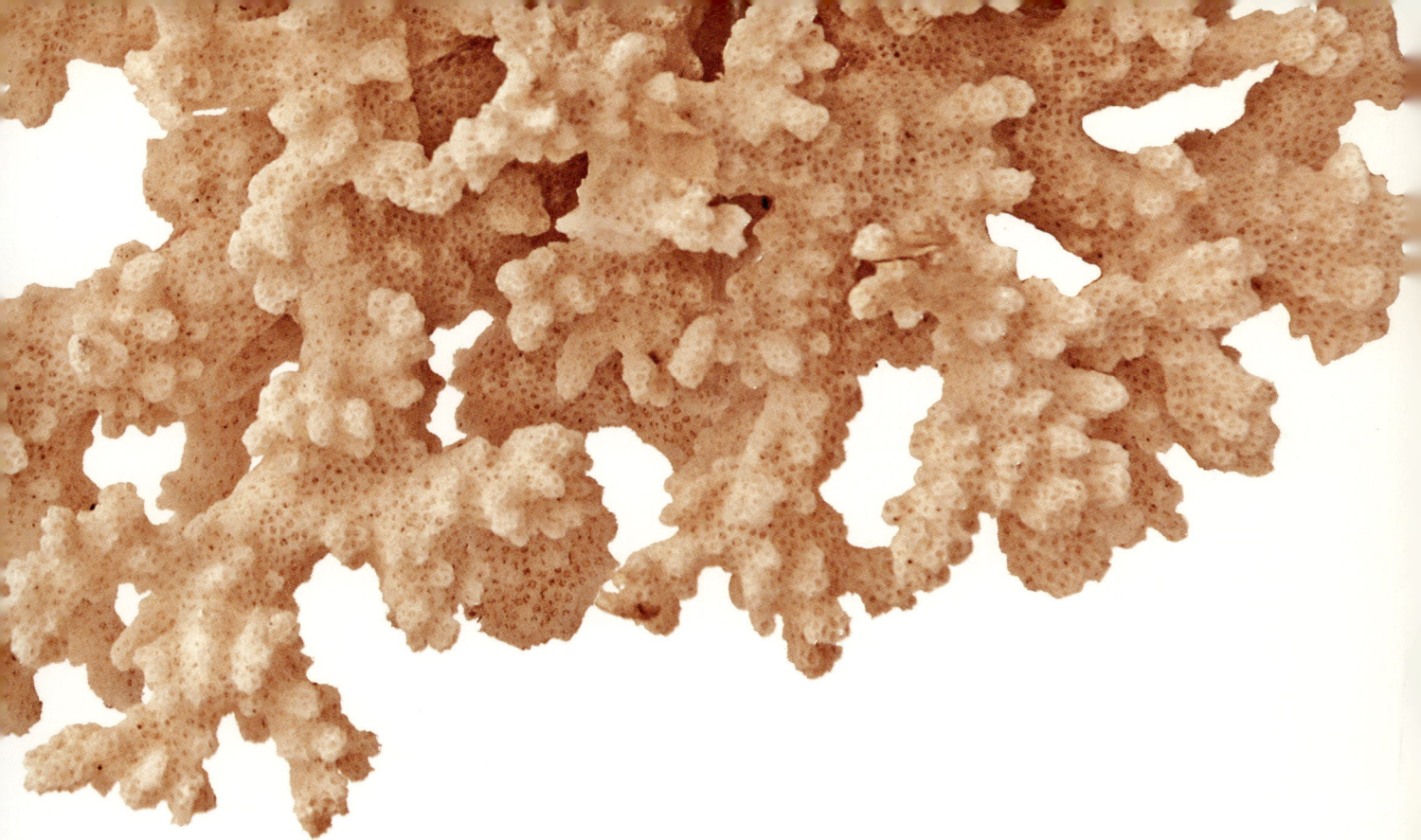

CONTENTS

ATLANTIC SPOTTED DOLPHINS
of Mayaguana

A nation in the southwestern Atlantic Ocean, the Bahamas consists of more than 700 islands. Mayaguana is the easternmost island of the Bahamas. It is about the size of Orlando, Florida, but has fewer than 300 human inhabitants. Forests are home to colorful birds such as vireos, warblers, and nighthawks as well as abundant lizards. Flamingos, pelicans, and boobies patrol the pristine beaches.

In the clear, blue waters off the eastern coast, coral reefs provide rich habitat for a multitude of creatures, from sponges and sea fans to barracudas, sharks, sea turtles, and dolphins. A family of Atlantic spotted dolphins has gathered along the edge of the reef. It is mid-May and a balmy 77 °F (25 °C). Something exciting is about to happen. For almost a year, a baby spotted dolphin has been growing inside its mother's body. The time has now come for it to be born.

Blowhole

A dolphin breathes through its blowhole, a type of nostril located on top of the head. At the surface, the dolphin opens its blowhole to quickly exhale and inhale fresh air. Then the blowhole automatically shuts.

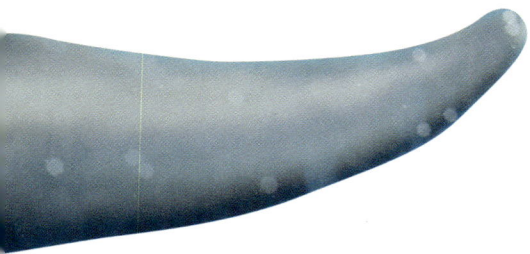

CHAPTER ONE

LIFE BEGINS

Dolphins are marine mammals. These are animals that live in the water, breathe air, give birth to fully formed young, and produce milk to feed them. Like all mammals, dolphins are warm-blooded. This means that their bodies maintain a constant temperature that is usually warmer than their surroundings. To stay warm, dolphins have a layer of fat, called blubber, just beneath the skin. About 20 percent of a dolphin's body weight is blubber. There are about 40 species of dolphin, though this number continues to change as new discoveries are made. Dolphins can be found in all the world's oceans and in some Asian and South American rivers. Most species prefer warm temperatures.

MAYAGUANA ATLANTIC SPOTTED DOLPHIN MILESTONES

DAY 1

- ▸ Born
- ▸ Skin a solid gray color, no spots
- ▸ Weight: 38 pounds (17.2 kg)
- ▸ Length: 32 inches (81.3 cm)

Welcome to the World

Off Mayaguana, the mother Atlantic spotted dolphin is swimming in broad circles, flexing her body. The members of her pod surround her, protecting her. A small tail emerges from the mother's body. In a few minutes, the rest of her baby slips into the water. He is about three feet (0.9 m) long. Momentarily unsure of himself, the wiggling calf begins to sink. His mother immediately circles around. She pushes the newborn toward the water's surface, where he takes his first breath of air.

The largest member of the dolphin family is the orca, or killer whale. The average male weighs about 10,000 pounds (4,536 kg) and is roughly 26 feet (7.9 m) long. Most other dolphin species range from 5 to 10 feet (1.5–3 m) long. Female dolphins are typically smaller than males. While adult orcas have no natural predators, other dolphins are hunted by orcas and sharks. Dolphins feed mostly on fish, squid, and shrimp. Some species have as many as 250 teeth, yet dolphins don't chew their food. They use their teeth to trap prey, and then they swallow it whole.

Dolphins live in groups called pods. Depending on food availability, pod size can vary from as few as five to hundreds of members. Adult males gather in separate pods from females. Dolphin mothers keep their young close at all times. Nursery pods consist of related females and their immature offspring. Because calves are not

FLUKE

DORSAL FIN

CLOSE-UP
Appendages

The side pectoral flippers help a dolphin slow down and steer. The dorsal fin, on the back, is used for balance. (Right whale dolphins lack that dorsal fin.) The tail, called the fluke, is used to propel a dolphin forward.

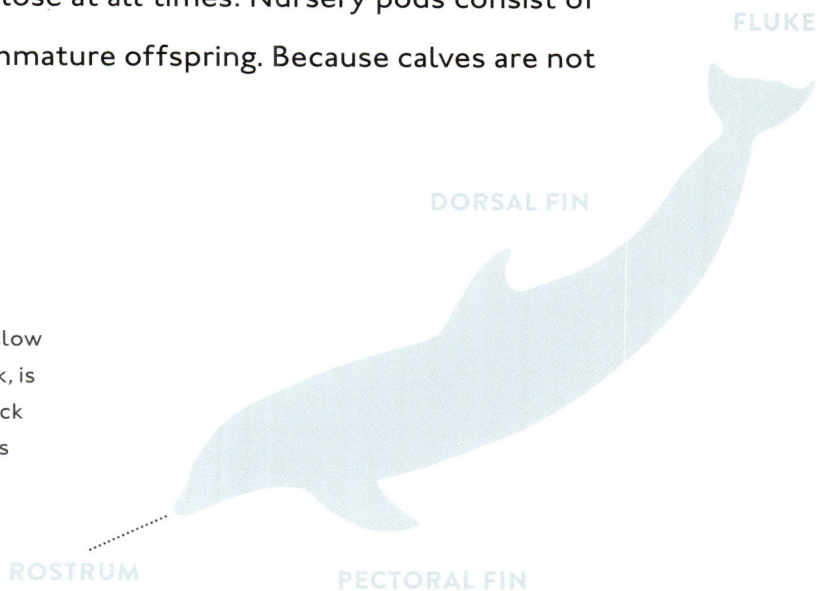

ROSTRUM

PECTORAL FIN

(2) WEEKS

▸ Flippers and fluke are stiff and strong

— FEATURED FAMILY —

First Meal

The calf cannot yet eat solid food. The inside of his jaws are soft, for he has no teeth. Those will not begin to erupt for two to three months. For now, he relies on his mother's milk. During feeding, mother and calf swim close to the water's surface. To feed, the calf pushes his snout through a slit in his mother's underbelly. He finds a nipple and forms a watertight "straw" with his flexible tongue. Then he pushes with his rostrum. This signals his mother to squirt her milk.

HOW LONG CAN A
DOLPHIN HOLD
ITS BREATH?

1-2 minutes | **BABY DOLPHIN**

10-15 minutes | **ADULT DOLPHIN**

strong swimmers, they ride pressure waves created by their mothers' swimming, like underwater surfing. Adults typically surface to breathe every 10 to 15 minutes. Young calves must come up for air every one or two minutes. To strengthen their breathing muscles, calves may chin slap: They raise their heads straight out of the water, take a big breath, and then slap their chins down, forcing air out of their blowholes. Mothers monitor their calves as they chin slap, nudging them to the surface when they slip too far below the waves.

2 **MONTHS**

▸ Begins socializing with other calves
▸ Remains at mother's side
▸ Weight: 83 pounds (37.6 kg)

3 **MONTHS**

▸ Teeth are erupting

Communication

Dolphins communicate and form social bonds by rubbing and nudging each other. They also whistle through their blowhole and click using a nasal sac in their forehead, called a melon. They can make squeaks, quacks, grunts, barks, and trills. Most dolphin sounds are too high-pitched to be heard by human ears.

CHAPTER TWO

EARLY ADVENTURES

Once they reach their teens, female dolphins typically give birth to one calf every two to three years. Twins are extremely rare. Members of nursery pods work together to teach and protect youngsters. However, roughly 20 percent of calves do not survive their first year. Many are sickened by parasites or pollution or attacked by predators. Communication is vital to dolphin survival. Using a language of whistles, clicks, and other sounds, dolphins form relationships, hunt cooperatively for food, and drive away enemies. Each dolphin has a signature whistle that it uses like a name to identify itself and be called by other dolphins.

(4) MONTHS

- ▸ Watches mother crater feed
- ▸ Learns by observing
- ▸ Practices hunting by playing with dead fish
- ▸ Weight: 128 pounds (58.1 kg)

Dolphins learn quickly and form memories. They are believed to be smarter than chimpanzees. Dolphins can use what they know and learn to solve problems. They share their knowledge and skills with their offspring and other pod members. Dolphins living in different habitats possess different skills for hunting and capturing prey. In mud-ring feeding, bottlenose dolphins swim in a circle in shallow water, kicking up mud with their tails to make a ring of cloudy plumes. Panicked fish leap over the plumes into the mouths of dolphins waiting outside the ring. In Patagonia, orcas rush up onto the beach during high tide to grab sea lion pups. Teams of dusky dolphins use vocalizations to corral anchovies into a tight ball. Then they rush through the ball and grab mouthfuls of the fish.

Eyesight

Dolphins have excellent vision. Their eyes can move independently of each other, allowing the dolphin to look in two different directions at once. Dolphins can also use both eyes together to focus and judge distance.

FEATURED FAMILY

Look Who's Leaping

In Mayaguana, the Atlantic spotted dolphin calf swims close to his mother's side, pulled along on the pressure wave created by her swimming. In this way, the calf uses about 90 percent less energy than his mother. He is now 6 months old and has grown 12 inches (30.5 cm) in length. He watches as his three-year-old brother and five-year-old sister leap out of the water. Keeping a close eye on his mother, the calf prepares to join them. With a burst of his tail, he pushes himself upward. He makes it halfway out of the water before bellyflopping. He is not nearly as strong as his older siblings. For now, he can only watch them play.

(6) **MONTHS**

▸ Begins feeding on fish and shrimp
▸ Develops hunting skills

▸ Weight: 165 pounds (74.8 kg)
▸ Length: 4 feet (1.2 m)

Echolocation

Dolphins send out high-pitched sound waves from their melon. These waves bounce off an object and return to the dolphin as an echo. This echo creates a mental picture of the size and shape of the object. Like an X-ray, echolocation can also be used to see inside things.

FEATURED FAMILY

Give It a Try

At nine months old, the calf is fully weaned. This means he no longer requires his mother's milk. He hunts for fish. One technique his mother has taught him is crater feeding. Using echolocation, the calf locates a pearly razorfish hiding under the sand. He positions his body vertically and begins to spin, his rostrum digging a crater into the sand. The calf then stuns the uncovered fish with a sound wave burst and snaps it up.

Dolphins are believed to be SMARTER than chimpanzees.

(9) **MONTHS**

- Fully weaned
- Weight: 200 pounds (90.7 kg)
- Length: 5 feet (1.5 m)

Teeth

Dolphins' teeth are cone-shaped and of uniform size. The teeth interlock, securely gripping prey. Dolphin teeth are permanent. Lost or broken teeth are not regrown.

CHAPTER THREE
LIFE LESSONS

River dolphins, found in freshwater and brackish habitats, are very different from their ocean-dwelling cousins. They are smaller and have no blubber. They live only about 15 to 20 years. Other dolphin species commonly live 30 to 50 years. River dolphins develop faster than other dolphins. They reach maturity between two and three years old, and when mothers say goodbye to their offspring, they typically never see them again. With no natural predators, river dolphins tend to live alone or in small groups of two or three.

Because of the many dangers in the open ocean, other dolphin species find safety in numbers. Orca pods are led by the oldest female. These pods are made up of several mothers and their offspring. The pod's 10 to 30 members travel together for their entire lives. Other

2 YEARS
- Begins to swim away from mother's side
- Joins in play with other young dolphins

3 YEARS
- Develops first spots on skin
- Joins mini pod of adolescent dolphins

FEATURED FAMILY

This Is How It's Done

Near the reef off Mayaguana, the spotted dolphin calf's siblings are babysitting. The dolphins spot a Caribbean reef octopus. The sister immediately grabs it. Her brothers follow her to the surface. The calf watches his sister leap and fling the octopus. It crashes down hard, its soft flesh pummeled by the impact. Next, the calf's brother grabs the octopus and leaps from the water. When he slams the octopus against the water's surface, its tender body falls to pieces. The calf has just learned how to break an octopus into bite-sized morsels.

oceanic dolphin pods frequently change. Between the ages of three and six years old, young dolphins leave their mother's side and swim in a subgroup of other adolescents. After some time in a subgroup, males leave their families and join all-male pods. Males typically come and go from different pods, but some form pair-bond relationships that can last for many years. Males reach maturity at 8 to 15 years old, depending on the species. They only briefly visit female pods to mate. Females remain in their mother's pod. They mate and begin raising babies of their own when they are 9 to 12 years old.

For young dolphins, living in a pod is like going to school. They learn cooperative hunting strategies. They develop social skills. Serving as

4 YEARS

- Serves as a babysitter to young calves
- Weight: 250 pounds (113 kg)
- Length: 6.5 feet (2 m)

6 YEARS

- Fully spotted skin
- Eating up to 30 pounds (13.6 kg) of fish a day

babysitters, they learn how to care for and protect younger dolphins. And they play with each other, which engages their natural curiosity and stimulates their brains. One "game" involves a group of dolphins tossing seaweed into the air, dragging it around in their mouths or on their flippers, and passing it to other dolphins. They also play catch with their prey, tossing fish around like a football.

CLOSE-UP
Mating rituals

When a female is selected for mating, her partner enlists the help of his friends to keep the activity private. Three or four trusted males will encircle the mating pair to ensure that no other dolphins try to steal the female away.

—— FEATURED FAMILY ——

Practice Makes Perfect

At dusk, a school of spotted lanternfish rises from the depths to feed on plankton. The spotted dolphin calf, now a year old, joins his family in bubble fishing. The dolphins encircle the lanternfish, whistling and blowing streams of bubbles from their blowholes. The bubbles surround the panicked fish. The school turns into a tight, swirling mass. Some dolphins hold the school in tight formation as others race up from below and fill their mouths with fish. In this manner, the dolphins—including the calf—take turns corralling and feeding.

PLAY
engages dolphins'
NATURAL
CURIOSITY
and *stimulates* their
BRAINS.

(9) **YEARS**

▸ Full-grown
▸ Leaves family to join adult males
▸ Weight: 315 pounds (143 kg)
▸ Length: 7.5 feet (2.3 m) long

(13) **YEARS**

▸ Mates for the first time

(40) **YEARS**

▸ End of life

CHAPTER FOUR

DOLPHIN SPOTTING

Some dolphin species are in trouble. River and coastal dolphins suffer habitat destruction. Chemicals that run into the water from factories and farms as well as sewage, oil, and other poisons pollute their homes. The baiji, also called the Yangtze River dolphin, was last seen in 2002. Scientists believe it is now **extinct**. The Chinese white dolphin shares its habitat with thousands of ships that collide with the dolphins and destroy their habitat. Ganges River dolphins live in one of the most polluted rivers on Earth. This species has decreased in number by nearly 70 percent in recent decades. Now, fewer than 2,000 exist in their native India.

In 2017, a new research project sponsored by World Wildlife Fund involved tagging a number of Amazon river dolphins so that their movements could be tracked. The data collected could help scientists devise better plans for preservation. Gold mining in the Amazon Basin has polluted the waters with deadly mercury, so scientists also plan to test and monitor dolphins' blood. Similar research has been conducted by the Indus River Dolphin Conservation Project in Pakistan.

Oceanic dolphins face a number of challenges as well. They often get caught in giant nets used for large-scale fishing. Maui's dolphin has suffered greatly from fishing nets. Fewer than 60 of these dolphins are believed to exist today. Dolphins also compete with humans for food—and humans are winning. People take about 66 million pounds (29.9 million kg) of fish out of the oceans every day! Learning what dolphins need to thrive is one way to help protect them. Scientists with Florida's Sarasota Dolphin Research Program have been studying dolphin behavior since 1970. They consider food resources and climate in relation to dolphin reproduction and success. Researchers also tag dolphins to track their movements, helping them better understand dolphins' habits.

Dolphin communication is a focus of study for Dr. Denise Herzing's Wild Dolphin Project. Since 1985, the project has studied Atlantic spotted dolphins. The organization has developed a sort of dictionary of dolphin sounds and is working on a computer-aided device that may allow humans to "speak" to dolphins in a language the animals can understand. Such research is vital to the preservation and protection of dolphins and their habitats for generations to come.

SNAPSHOTS

Given the Māori name for New Zealand's North Island, **Maui's dolphin** is also called *popoto*. It is the smallest known dolphin species.

The **La Plata dolphin** lives in brackish coastal waters where rivers in southern South America empty into the Atlantic Ocean.

The **Burrunan dolphin** of Australia was classified as a new species in 2011. Only about 150 individuals are known to exist.

The **striped dolphin** has dived as deep as 2,200 feet (671 m) while hunting and can leap more than 20 feet (6.1 m) into the air.

Generations of mating between spinner and striped dolphins led to the emergence of a new species. The **Clymene dolphin** was officially recognized in 1981.

The **endangered Irrawaddy dolphin** lives near coasts and in estuaries of the Bay of Bengal and Southeast Asia.

Commerson's dolphin of coastal southern Argentina is nicknamed the "panda dolphin" or "skunk dolphin" for its striking black-and-white coloration.

Pacific white-sided dolphins inhabit the cool waters of the northern Pacific, where their main predator is the **orca**.

The **melon-headed whale** is a rarely seen dolphin that lives far from shore in all the world's warm oceans.

The **Amazon river dolphin**, also called *boto*, has a flexible neck to help it maneuver through tangles of underwater plants and tree roots.

Spinner dolphins have 250 teeth, the most of any mammal. They are also the only dolphins to naturally leap from the water in corkscrews.

The **hourglass dolphin**, which inhabits the frigid Southern Ocean, is named for the markings on its body.

About 150 **false killer whales** live in Hawaiian waters. In 2012, they were listed as an endangered species.

WORDS to Know

brackish   containing a mixture of salt and fresh water

endangered   at risk of dying out completely

extinct   died off completely; having no living members

parasites   animals or plants that live on or inside another living thing (called a host) while giving nothing back to the host; some parasites cause disease or even death

plankton   tiny plants and animals that drift or float in the ocean; many are microscopic

rostrum   a stiff, beaklike snout extending from an animal's head

species   a group of living beings with shared characteristics and the ability to reproduce with one another

LEARN MORE

Books

Casey, Susan. *Dolphins: Voices in the Ocean.* New York: Delacorte Press, 2018.

Dipper, Frances. *Pocket Guide to Whales, Dolphins, and Other Marine Mammals.* London: Frances Lincoln Children's Books, 2018.

Szymanski, Jennifer. *In the Ocean.* Washington, D.C.: National Geographic Children's Books, 2018.

Websites

"Basic Facts about Dolphins." Defenders of Wildlife. https://defenders.org /dolphin/basic-facts.

"Facts about Dolphins." Whale and Dolphin Conservation (WDC). https://us.whales.org/whales-dolphins/facts-about-dolphins.

"Orca." National Geographic. https://www.nationalgeographic.com/animals /mammals/o/orca/.

Documentaries

Chisholm, Suzanne, and Michael Parfit. *The Whale.* Mountainside Films and Téléfilm Canada, 2011.

Ellena, Eric. *The Mystery of the Pink Dolphin.* French Connection Films, DUO2, and Institut de Recherche pour le Développement, 2015.

Fothergill, Alastair, and Keith Scholey. *Dolphins.* Disneynature and Silverback Films, 2018.

Note: Every effort has been made to ensure that any websites listed above were active at the time of publication. However, because of the nature of the Internet, it is impossible to guarantee that these sites will remain active indefinitely or that their contents will not be altered.

Visit

BIRCH AQUARIUM WHALE WATCHING

Adventurous visitors may see gray whales, porpoises, and dolphins in the wild.

2300 Expedition Way
La Jolla, CA 92037

THE DOLPHIN EXPLORER

Led by Coast Guard specialists, visitors get close-up interaction with wild dolphins.

Marco River Marina
951 Bald Eagle Drive
Marco Island, FL 34145

NATIONAL AQUARIUM DOLPHIN DISCOVERY

This site is home to a family of Atlantic bottlenose dolphins.

501 East Pratt Street
Baltimore, MD 21202

ORCA SPIRIT ADVENTURES

Visitors can see orca pods in the wild.

950 Wharf Street (November to April)
146 Kingston Street, Marina Level
(April to November)
Victoria, BC
Canada V8V 1V4

INDEX